A transitional boneshaker, about 1869. This machine in the author's collection has wooden wheels of 38 inches (1 m) and 22 inches (560 mm) diameter. Riders found that it was more effective to get their weight over the front wheel and that a larger wheel could give faster speeds.

EARLY BICYCLES

Nick Clayton

Shire Publications Ltd

CONTENTS

Published in 1994 by Shire Publications Ltd, Cromwell House, Church Street, Princes Risborough, Buckinghamshire HP27 9AJ, UK. Copyright © 1986 and 1994 by Nick Clayton. First edition 1986; reprinted with amendments 1990 and 1994. Shire Album 173. ISBN 0 85263 803 5.

Printed in Great Britain by CIT Printing Services, Press Buildings, Merlins Bridge,Haverfordwest, Dyfed SA61 1XF.

British Library Cataloguing in Publication Data: Clayton, Nick. Early bicycles. – (Shire album; 173) 1. Bicycles – History. I. Title. 629. 2'272'09034 TL400. ISBN 0-85263-803-5.

COVER: *A fashion plate depicting a Victorian family out for a ride on tricycles, from 'Illustrations of British Costumes', published in 1889 by the John Williamson Company, Drury Lane, London.*

BELOW: *Karl von Drais, 1785-1851, the inventor of the first bicycle.*

ACKNOWLEDGEMENTS

I am indebted to Peter W. Card for contributing the chapter on accessories and to Roger Street for his invaluable assistance with the chapter on tricycles.

Illustrations are acknowledged to: Birmingham Museum of Science and Industry, pages 20 (lower), 22 (upper), 25 (lower); Christchurch Tricycle Museum, page 23 (left); N. G. Clayton and Glynn Stockdale, page 1; CTC Archives, page 10; David Feakes, page 27; Glasgow Museum of Transport, page 18; M. J. Kelsey, page 6; Mark Hall Cycle Museum, page 16 (upper); Musée National des Techniques, page 7; Museum of British Road Transport, page 13 (upper); National Cycle Museum, page 17; Tom Norton, page 12; John Pinkerton, pages 9 (upper), 15; Science Museum, pages 5, 8, 11, 13 (lower), 22 (lower), 23 (right), 24 (centre and bottom), 25 (upper), 26; Glynn Stockdale, page 9 (lower); Tangent and Coventry Tricycle Company catalogue, page 24 (top); Ulster Folk and Transport Museum, pages 4, 16 (lower), 19, 20 (upper), 21; University of Ulm, pages 2, 3; *Wheeling* magazine, page 29. The photograph on page 14 is by the author.

Karl von Drais patented his 'Laufmaschine' (running machine) in 1817. Made mainly of wood and weighing 40 pounds (18 kg), it was propelled by the rider's feet striking the ground on either side. The rider's elbows rested on the upholstered balance board. There was space behind the rider for a portmanteau.

INTRODUCTION

The bicycle developed over the seventy-five year period from 1817 to 1892 and the story is full of colourful characters and bizarre inventions. It is easy to be distracted by the curious and whimsical thereby missing the truly successful developments. Of any new improvement the Victorians asked the question, 'Does it answer?' It seems reasonable to conclude that the bulk of the machines which survive today represent the ones which did, whilst those that exist only in the patent records and in the pages of the books and magazines of the day did not.

In the development of the bicycle five major innovations stand above the thousands of minor improvements which have led to the modern cycle.

1817: Baron von Drais of Karlsruhe invented the hobby-horse.
1864: Michaux sells pedal-driven velocipedes in Paris.
1869: Meyer of Paris perfected the suspension wheel.
1884: J. K. Starley of Coventry introduced the Rover rear-driven 'safety' bicycle.
1888: J. B. Dunlop of Belfast patented the pneumatic tyre.

In following this progression it must be concluded that in the long term both the Ordinary and the tricycle were blind alleys, but they attracted a huge army to the pastime of cycling and bridged the gap between the boneshaker and the safety bicycle. It seems very possible that if the suspension or spider wheel had not been forthcoming in 1869 velocipede mania would have died out in the same way that the hobby-horse craze had died forty years before, but the spider-wheeled Ordinary captured the hearts of thousands who rode it. Tens of thousands came to watch the new sport of cycle racing and, as happened in later years with both motorcycles and motorcars, it was racing which provided the catalyst for improvement in machines.

The success of a particular maker and his professional jockeys largely determined which new model won the allegiance of the club rider. When the Ordinary was finally deposed by the solid-tyred rear-driven 'safety' and that in its turn was superseded by the pneumatic safety, it was success on the road and path which encouraged the public to take up the new machines.

DATING GUIDE

Hobby-horse	1817 - 20
Boneshaker or velocipede	1868 - 72
Ordinary (Penny farthing)	1870 - 92
Dwarf safety (Kangaroo)	1884 - 86
Tricycle	1876 - 95
Rear-driven safety (solid tyre)	1884 - 92
Geared front driver (GO)	1889 - 96
Cross-frame safety	1884 - 92
Pneumatic safety	1890 - present

Denis Johnson of Long Acre, London, took out a patent for a machine which was very similar to the Draisenne on 21st December 1818. Light, with elegant iron stays and forks, the backbone curved down in the middle to allow the use of larger wheels which reduced rolling resistance. Johnson operated one of the first velocipede riding schools.

4

One of the most famous bicycles but perhaps the least significant in its influence on future developments is in the Science Museum, London. It was made about 1860 by Thomas McCall 'after the pattern' of one constructed around 1839 by Kirkpatrick Macmillan of Dumfries. The rear driving principle was not generally adopted for a further forty years.

MANUMOTIVES, HOBBIES AND QUADRICYCLES

About the middle of the eighteenth century amateur engineers began experimenting with man-powered conveyances. The usual method was for servants to supply the motive power either by hand cranks (manumotives) or foot treadles (pedomotives). These vehicles were based on the light carriage of the day and had three or four wheels. The concept of balancing on two wheels was not one that would easily occur to minds which had experience only of multi-wheeled vehicles.

There was genius, then, in the invention by Baron Karl von Drais of Karlsruhe of a two-wheeled machine with both wheels in line, for which he took out a patent in 1817. This machine, soon christened the hobby-horse or dandy-horse, became an instant craze in London, Paris, Calcutta and many of the world's capitals. It was copied in England by Denis Johnson of London and others.

Propulsion was achieved simply by pushing with the feet on the ground and to facilitate this in reasonable comfort the saddle height was adjustable and a padded board was fitted behind the handles for balancing the machine with the elbows. Foot rests were sometimes fitted to the front forks for coasting downhill, but because there was no mechanical means of propulsion the conveyance was only really practical in parks or on level ground. It appears that von Drais, who was a prolific inventor in other fields, was inspired by the concept of skating without ice. The new sport, taken up so enthusiastically by the dandies in 1818, had run its course within a couple of years, and when in 1832 von Drais visited England with an improved design he appears to have been largely ignored.

Hobby-horses were extensively copied in the intervening years and although there were significant differences between von Drais's machine and Johnson's, particularly in the steering arrangement, it is difficult, where there is no maker's plate, to attribute the few surviving machines to any particular maker.

After 1820 interest again concentrated on quadricycles and tricycles but of the many models suggested or actually built only one or two had commercial success. The most prolific maker of quadricycles was Willard Sawyer of Dover. Sawyer's machines were light and elegant (58 pounds, 26 kg) with wooden wheels and frame, usually propelled via slippers and treadles with a cranked rear axle. The front wheels were steered by a tiller. A single-seater ridden by an enthusiast was capable of up to sixty miles per day and Sawyer made them in several different models from 1845 for over twenty years. Necessarily expensive, the number found in museums today probably reflects the care their original owners took with them rather than any high volume production.

Whilst the mechanism of the crank was being utilised both directly and indirectly for multi-wheeled machines, the idea that it could be employed to propel a hobby-horse so that one might balance on two wheels whilst pedalling was one that eluded inventors for over forty years unless one accepts the claims made on behalf of a Dumfries blacksmith, Kirkpatrick Macmillan. In 1839 he made a wooden-wheeled machine which may have been driven by levers attached to cranks on the rear axle. As only later reconstructions of this machine now exist and there are no contemporary drawings, it is hard to evaluate the claim. Whatever the case the idea was not transmitted to a wider public.

Between the hobby-horse of 1818 and the boneshaker of 1869 most of the interest in velocipedes was in quadricycles. Willard Sawyer of Dover was the foremost manufacturer, operating from about 1845. This photograph, taken about 1872, shows two gentlemen on front-driving, rear-steering machines.

The first commercial pedal-driven bicycle was made by Michaux of Paris with a wrought-iron serpentine-shaped frame similar to the Johnson hobby horse of 1818. French velocipedes were imported into England in late 1868, creating a demand which led to the establishment of the British cycle industry.

THE VELOCIPEDE OR BONESHAKER

The vital development which gave the bicycle its own means of propulsion happened in Paris in the mid 1860s. Debate continues as to exactly how this occurred but by 1867 the new toy was all the rage.

Michaux et Compagnie was the first and largest manufacturer of these machines, which were propelled by cranks fitted to the front axle, although the only patent obtained was by Pierre Lallement in 1866 in the USA. Lallement was later said to have made his first machine in Paris in 1863. By the summer of 1868 the craze had reached New York and in November the first machines arrived at Spencer's gymnasium in London. In 1869 velocipedomania erupted in England too but within two years the craze had passed.

The Michaux company was controlled by two brothers, René and Aimé Olivier. These energetic young men, keen velocipedists, improved the design, financed factories, wrote promotional tracts and arranged publicity events, including the first road race from Paris to Rouen. In April 1869 they bought the remaining shares in the company and changed the name to La Compagnie Parisienne des Velocipedes. Unfortunately, like the other French makers, their early entrepreneurship did not reappear after the Franco-Prussian war.

Early Michaux machines had a serpentine-shaped frame like the hobby horse but in 1868 they patented a diagonal frame which was more rigid and saved weight. Most surviving machines, of which there are a surprising number, follow this type. The American Pickering bicycle was a similar pattern but used hydraulic tubing for lightness: this was the first use of tubing in cycle manufacture.

Despite their brief tenure boneshakers were often well engineered and carried attractive detailing. The best wheels had elm stocks, hickory spokes and ash felloes (rims) bent in one piece so that they required only one joint. Bronze axle bushes which needed lubrication with whale oil would be fitted with brass oil reservoirs. Saddles, pedals, foot rests and lamp brackets, reflecting their carriage trade ancestry, were sometimes highly ornamental despite the weight penalty. The average boneshaker weighed about 60 pounds (27 kg) and could sustain around 8 miles per hour (13 km/h).

At first the approved riding position was with the saddle equidistant between the wheels, the instep resting on the pedals, the arms outstretched on the wide handles and the body leaning slightly backwards. This allowed for good control of the machine when descending hills, but was inefficient in ascent and tiring even on level ground. In addition the small diameter of the front wheel, usually 36 inches (910 mm), produced an unpleasantly fast pedalling cadence and the iron-shod wheel would slip on loose surfaces. Attempts to gear up the front wheel using spur gears failed due to the inefficiency of hand-cut gears and lack of rigidity in the bearings.

Mounting an early velocipede was an athletic achievement. The manuals advised running beside the machine and

vaulting into the saddle, a daunting task for the tyro. However, later models were fitted with a step suspended from the frame which enabled the rider to coast before mounting or dismounting, a much more relaxed procedure. The historian Bartleet claims this invention for James Starley of the Coventry Machinists Company Limited but there is no Starley patent of the feature.

Pedals were at first simple bobbins with flanges to hold the instep. The first improvement was a flat pedal with a counterweight or plumb bob which always presented a flat face to the foot. The plumb bob was often in the form of an acorn or pineapple. Finally a simple triangular pedal was found to serve the purpose effectively. Different leg lengths were accommodated, at first by having two or three fixing holes for the pedal pin and later by slotting the cranks for variable adjustment. Curved leg rests, often leather-covered for comfort, on a projection over the front wheel, were for use when coasting downhill.

Braking was achieved by back pedalling or with the assistance of a spoon brake acting on the face of the rear wheel. The brake was applied by levers, or by revolving the handlebar and so tightening a connecting cord. As this arrangement was not fail-safe steep hills presented a risk if the cord broke.

Another inconvenience of the velo-

A Pickering boneshaker of 1869, imported from New York to Liverpool. This was one of the first bicycles with spares made 'to gauge' and so did not require fitting. This machine, now in the Pinkerton Collection, lacks the brake pad attached to the rear of the saddle which was applied by the rider leaning backwards.

cipede was the way that the front wheel cleaned itself on the rider's trousers when turning corners. Unsuccessful attempts were made to remedy this defect with machines hinged between the wheels (the Phantom) and rear-steering machines. Both proved less stable than front-steerers and were consequently short-lived, although the Phantom, with its early form of suspension wheel and rubber tyre, was appreciated for its lightness compared with wooden-wheeled machines.

The invention of the step allowed riders to mount machines with larger driving wheels and in 1869 wooden-wheeled machines were being offered with a front wheel diameter as large as 48 inches (1.22 m). To manage such a wheel it was necessary to sit well forward, almost over the front axle, in order to reach the pedals. Apart from improving the gearing by covering more ground with each turn of the pedals, this position had the added benefit that the weight of the body could be used to propel the machine instead of relying on the strength of the arms and legs alone.

This improvement coincided with the development of the wire-spoked suspension wheel, which probably did as much as did the invention of the crank to establish the bicycle as a serious means of transport. The credit is usually given to

An English boneshaker, about 1869. Although the French boneshakers were considered the best, English makers quickly started producing quality machines. The maker of this machine operated a general iron foundry in Salford.

9

THE PATENT VELOCIPEDE

"EAGLE."

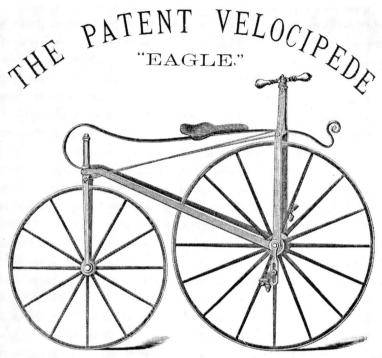

STASSEN & CO'S.
PATENT VELOCIPEDE.

1st—Advantages of this Velocipede over all others is that it is guided by the back wheel, thereby obviating the annoyance felt by all riders of having the front wheel grinding their legs at the slightest turn.

2nd—Being fitted with a cam in the back fork, the machine has a self acting tendancy whilst working to keep in a direct line, thus preventing in a measure the rolling so unsightly in all other machines.

3rd—The front or driving wheel being always square with the body of the rider, your feet are not likely to slip off the pedals, and it is impossible to get your leg between the ironwork and the wheel.

4th—Being lighter than the other form of Velocipedes it requires less work, at the same time from its formation, it is stronger and more adapted for carrying parcels.

CLASS A.

Best American Hickory Wheels, Gunmetal bushed. Forged from S.C. Iron, Steel Spring and Pigskin Saddle:

Up to 36 in. driving wheel	£10	0	0
From 36 in. to 38 in. ,, ...	£11	0	0
,, 38 in. to 40 in. ,, ...	£12	0	0

CLASS B.

Similar to A but with brass triangular pedals, brass Break, polished spring, No. 1. Pigskin Saddle, and extra fine painted, **£2 5s.** each extra.

Match Machines with polished wheels and ironwork, fitted with oil tubes, oil can, and spanner in case, **£18 18s.**

The above prices are applicable to the regular pattern Velocipede of the same sizes.

STASSEN & Co., ENGINEERS,
237, EUSTON ROAD.

ABOVE: *The Phantom, 1869. The central hinge overcame the problem of the front wheel catching the rider's leg when cornering but demanded what a horseman would call 'good hands' to keep it on a straight course. It was one of the earliest models to have wire spokes, tensioned by driving the hub flanges apart.*

OPPOSITE: *The Eagle boneshaker. A familiar complaint amongst velocipedists was that the front wheel caught their leg when cornering. Several rear steering patterns were tried but with little success. The Eagle was short-lived but Stassen continued as a successful manufacturer of both Ordinaries and safeties.*

Meyer of Paris who patented in August 1869 a wheel which allowed for the spokes to be tightened individually by nuts at the hub. The Coventry Machinists Company Limited had a pair of these wheels sent over from Paris and spider wheels with light, iron V-shaped rims and solid rubber tyres were soon adopted by all manufacturers. Wooden-wheeled machines were soon abandoned or used simply for learning on.

Although there were fifty or more firms offering velocipedes in England and over one hundred in France it is virtually impossible to attribute surviving machines from styling features alone. Happily many machines carry the maker's name on a brass plate or stamped into the rear of the seat spring.

By the end of 1870 enthusiasm for the velocipede had died down. The unreasonable weight resulting from the iron frame and wooden wheels made it more of a novelty than a practical means of transport. Public interest was not maintained and over the next few years, which saw the development and refinement of the Ordinary, interest was sustained only by the racing men and touring club enthusiasts.

Perhaps the most famous and best loved Ordinary bicycle, the Ariel with its lever tension wheel was patented by James Starley on 11th August 1870. It was made under licence by Haynes and Jefferis and remained in production for nearly ten years. This fine early example is in the Tom Norton collection at Llandrindod Wells.

THE ORDINARY

By the close of the 1870 season the boneshaker was becoming obsolete and the high wheeled Ordinary bicycle had begun its fifteen year reign. It was known as the Ordinary simply to differentiate it from the many and varied attempts at producing a satisfactory safety bicycle. After the safety bicycle was finally realised in 1885 the 'Grand Old Ordinary' was relinquished only reluctantly by its adherents and continued in production until 1892. It was only then, when it was becoming a rare sight on the road, that the term 'Penny farthing' was coined.

It sometimes seems strange that sixteen years and 200,000 Ordinaries separate the boneshaker and the Rover safety bicycle. It was certainly not because geared-up, rear-driving machines had not been thought of; there were many attempts to popularise such machines. Nor was it, as some have suggested,

because riders refused to accept change. From a very early period every manufacturer introduced annual model changes which were eagerly evaluated by the riding fraternity. The answer can perhaps best be discovered by riding a good Ordinary over an indifferent road. It coped well with the mud, dust and minor potholes which were the order of the day. Only occasionally did it throw its rider and as most of these were young, middle-class and male a few battle scars were considered acceptable. Club riders were very competitive. Out in all weathers and at all hours they vied with each other to clock up longer and longer distances, faster and faster times.

The Ordinary developed between 1870 and 1878. Scores of patents were taken out for rigid spoking systems, front and rear brakes, seat springs, pedals and bearings. Above all machines were made

A Humber racer. Most makers had a racing model in their catalogues but a few models like Invincible and Keen predominated. Humber was also in the forefront of racing success and was advertised in 1887 as the fastest bicycle in the world, 1 mile (1.6 km) having been ridden in 2 minutes 30 seconds.

free-running and lighter. The standard weight for the 1878 season was 'pounds for inches' that is to say a 50 inch (1.27 m) touring bicycle would weigh 50 pounds (23 kg) or less. Racing machines were even lighter, down to about 25 pounds (11 kg) and the James racer of 1888 weighed an incredible 11 pounds (5 kg). Speed records were regularly improved every season and on a 60 inch (1.52 m) Invincible H. L. Cortis became in 1882 the first man to cover 20 miles (32 km) within one hour.

Four models set the standard by which the early machines were judged. They were the Spider, later renamed the Gentleman's, made by the Coventry Machinists Company Limited; the Ariel made by

A Grout Tension, about 1871. Whilst the French must be credited with developing the boneshaker it was the English who led in perfecting the Ordinary. Many of the early patents were concerned with maintaining a true tensioned wheel. Grout solved the problem with threaded eyelets which allowed each spoke to be tightened individually. The saddle has gone from this Science Museum example.

1878 represented the full flowering of the Ordinary and the Club model introduced by Coventry Machinists Company Limited in that year was the classic touring bicycle. The frame was made of tapered oval steel tube which 'combines in a marked degree rigidity, strength, lightness and elegance'. This 56 inch (1.42 m) model dates from about 1885.

Haynes and Jefferis; the Tension patented by W. H. J. Grout of Stoke Newington and the Keen by John Keen of South Norwood. One man played a major role in developing the first two of these machines and was responsible for many other improvements during the 1870s. He was James Starley, christened by his peers 'the father of the cycle trade'.

The Club model which succeeded the Gentleman's in 1878 represents the classic Ordinary, recognised not only for its speed and utility but also for its beauty of line. The oval spine closely followed the curve of the front wheel, the small wheel was tucked in behind the large one, and all components including the rims were refined and made hollow to save unnecessary weight. After this date the annual model changes continued but perhaps only the wider cowhorn bars (1882) and true tangent spokes (1885) were significant improvements. When,

after 1885, the runaway success of the Rover rear-driven safeties began to affect the sales of Ordinaries, manufacturers tried to fight back by making a 'safe' machine. Known as Rationals these machines had a larger rear wheel, 22 inches (560 mm) against 16 or 18 inches (410 or 450 mm), more rake to the front forks and more clearance between the tyre and the backbone. For a few years they had some success and on the racing path if not on the road Ordinaries continued to excel until 1892. After this date manufacture of high bicycles virtually ceased.

Braking was an important consideration for Ordinary riders. Some chose to rely on the fixed wheel alone and to dismount when a hill appeared too steep. Most preferred the assistance of a brake, for in the right conditions it allowed one to coast down hills 'legs over'. The practice of putting the legs over the handlebar when coasting was adopted after some fearful accidents in the early 1870s. These were often precipitated by the feet becoming entangled in the spokes when using the small toe rests which opened out from the forks. The early brakes followed boneshaker practice of using a pad or roller on the rear wheel applied by a cord, but when the rear wheel became smaller and more of the rider's weight was placed over the front wheel, braking became less effective. The spoon brake on the front wheel, first introduced by John Keen in 1873, came into general use after 1879.

The other major development concerned the seat spring. Boneshakers needed a very pliable spring but the larger, rubber-tyred wheel of the Ordinary was more flexible and therefore a stiffer spring was adopted. As with boneshakers the maker's name is often found stamped on the rear of the seat spring. Over five hundred firms made Ordinaries. Coventry was the centre of the industry with other concentrations in Wolverhampton, Sheffield, Nottingham and London. Many names such as Singer, Humber, Hillman, Rudge and Ariel continued through safety manufacture into the motorcycle and motorcar era.

The 'Rational' Ordinary was shown at the 1886 Stanley Show by a small London maker, J. H. Dearlove. He claimed it was 'for riders who have had half the life shaken out of them through riding the modern boneshaker' (the Rover type 'safety'). With more rake, thick rubber tyres, long saddle and larger back wheel it was copied by all the major makers and delayed the demise of the Ordinary until the pneumatic tyre finally made the safety bicycle comfortable.

THE FACILE SAFETY BICYCLE

OPPOSITE, ABOVE: *Keen's Eclipse. John Keen was world champion in 1872, 1873 and 1874. Refined by his own racing experience, his bicycles were models of elegant simplicity. This beautiful example from about 1875 is in Mark Hall Cycle Museum, Harlow.*

OPPOSITE, BELOW: *One of the two successful front-wheel lever-driven bicycles, the Facile was ungeared yet prodigious distances were achieved on it. The rider applied his weight behind the hub so accidents were much less frequent. Invented in 1878 it was popular until the late 1880s.*

BELOW: *Unique in that it was neither bicycle nor tricycle, the Otto dicycle was first patented in 1877. The small rear castor was to prevent overbalancing, whilst steering was achieved by braking one of the wheels and thus slipping the driving band. This one is on display at the National Cycle Museum, Lincoln.*

The Singer Xtraordinary, patented in 1878, employed levers but usually had a larger driving wheel than the Facile. Unlike an Ordinary, the height of the pedals could be adjusted to suit the rider's leg length. This well preserved example is in the Glasgow Museum of Transport.

LEVERS, DWARFS AND DICYCLES

Simply because of its huge success the Ordinary created a demand from the more cautious and less athletic for a safer if less efficient machine. Plain spur gears having been tried and found wanting, two methods of seating the rider closer to the ground found acceptance. First levers were used and then later chain gears. Of the many lever-driven machines that were marketed only two had consistent success, the Facile and the Xtraordinary.

The Facile, invented by Beale and Straw in 1878, used levers pivoted from extensions of the forks below the hub. The foot action, instead of being circular, followed an arc, and once this had been mastered surprising distances could be achieved on a relatively small wheel. In 1883 Faciles broke the twenty-four-hour record five times, culminating in J. H. Adams's ride of 242 miles (384 km). In 1888 this was raised to 297 miles (472 km).

The Xtraordinary Challenge also used levers but with the pivot point halfway up the forks. Made by Singer and Company of Coventry it came out in 1879. The foot pressure was applied behind and below the hub and it was claimed to be 'safe even for night riding, regardless of such petty annoyances as scattered stones or a brick or two lying about, even a stray dog will be got over safely'. Together with tricycles these two models dominated the safety market until the dwarf front-driving machine arrived in 1884.

First produced by Hillman, Herbert and Cooper as the Kangaroo, the design with sprockets fixed on extensions to the forks and a chain drive to the hub was widely copied by almost all the leading manufacturers for the following season.

Chain technology had been developed on the early tricycles and the facility to gear it up by fitting different sized sprockets made the Kangaroo a winner both on the path and on the road. For two seasons it looked as though the dwarf front-driver might take over the position held for so long by the Ordinary but its success, although impressive, was fleeting and the rear-driven safety had removed it from the catalogues by 1888. Although the Kangaroo was often talked about as a safety machine the description is inaccurate as 'the upright forks and small back wheel rendered a cropper quite as easy of occurrence as on an Ordinary'.

Ellis and Company continued to make and sell the Facile against the new competitors and in 1887 developed a front-driving machine with sun and planet gearing. The crypto-geared Ordinary or G O helped to extend the joys of Ordinary riding for a few extra years and when fitted in 1891/2 with pneumatic tyres it was a rival to the true racing Ordinary. A small wheeled version of the geared ordinary known as the Crypto Bantam was marketed for several years to older riders who refused to accept the inevitability of the rear-driven safeties.

A singular exercise in designing the perfect safety machine, 'neither bicycle nor tricycle', was patented by E.C.T. Otto in 1877. Known as the 'dicycle' and its adherents as 'Ottoists', it survived despite the financial setbacks of its promoter for almost ten years during which time nearly one thousand were sold. An 1882 review said 'novices experience a strong inclination to pitch out forward on first applying pressure to the pedals.' Despite this shortcoming it was the first two-wheeled machine to be advertised as particularly suitable for ladies.

The dwarf front driver appeared in 1884 and many companies rushed out their own versions to take a share of the new market. The most famous was the Kangaroo made by Hillman, Herbert and Cooper and the name has become generic for this short-lived class of machine.

ABOVE: *The crypto-geared Ordinary was a successor to the Facile employing a sun-and-planet hub gear which enabled the front wheel to be geared up. Although perhaps not beautiful, these rare bicycles must have been splendid riding machines when fitted with Dunlop's pneumatic tyre in the early 1890s. This unrestored example is in Ulster Folk and Transport Museum.*

LEFT: *The Crypto Bantam was the small brother of the crypto-geared Ordinary although it could be geared up to suit the customer. Popular with older riders in the mid 1890s, they are a favoured mount for lady veteran riders today.*

A Dublin tricycle. The new spider wheels of the early 1870s allowed designers to build lightweight three-wheeled machines for potential cyclists who could not accept the Ordinary. William Blood was the first manufacturer, in 1876.

TRICYCLES

The tricycle was the alternative mount for those who were of the wrong age, temperament, physique or sex to ride the Ordinary. Between 1876 and 1892 tricycling attracted thousands of adherents who saw themselves as somehow superior to the common run of bicyclists. At the Stanley Show of 1883, 289 tricycles were on exhibition and the bicycles numbered only 233.

Boneshaker tricycles had been made and a few survive today, but they were heavy, unstable mounts and after the demise of the wooden-wheeled machines few tricycles were produced until 1876. In that year William Blood of Dublin patented the first of the new breed of spider-wheeled tricycles and this was closely followed by the Coventry Lever tricycle produced by the ubiquitous James Starley. A heavy man himself, Starley was sympathetic to the demands of the less agile and did as much as any

other individual to bring the tricycle to perfection.

The Coventry Lever tricycle incorporated Starley's patent tangent spokes. It was a two track machine with one large 50 inch (1.27 m) driving wheel in the middle of one side and two smaller wheels fore and aft, both of which were steerable. Propulsion was at first by levers and the steering via a tiller. Later, with rotary cranks and rack and pinion steering, it became well known and loved as the Coventry Rotary and then the Rudge Rotary. In 1877 Starley added a second large wheel at the side and, with a second seat and set of pedals, created the Coventry Sociable, the first sociable tricycle. It employed two driving wheels and early instability problems led Starley to add a balance gear or differential which allowed the two wheels to revolve at different speeds when cornering. Although not an original concept its

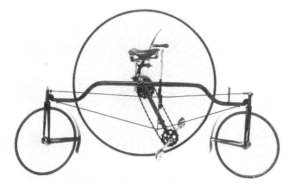

The Rudge Rotary tricycle. This is the further development of the Coventry Lever machine which gave a boost to the newly merged companies of Rudge, Smith Starley and Company, and Haynes and Jefferis, in 1880. Although chain transmission was employed it remained ungeared. Steering was by rack and pinion. Birmingham Museum of Science and Industry has this well restored example.

adaptation to the driving wheels of light vehicles made it perhaps the most far reaching invention of the tricycle age.

The Salvo was the first machine to incorporate Starley's balance gear and also the first successful application of the chain drive to cycles (thus helping to establish the fortune of Hans Renold who had just patented a new form of chain employing anti-friction bushes and rollers). This was a class of machine at last which women could ride without public disapproval.

There was a flurry of tricycle designs in the late 1870s with dozens of different patterns being tried. The Humber introduced in 1880 was particularly successful with its bicycle-handlebar steering of the two large front driving wheels. The layout with two large rear driving wheels and one small front steering wheel was at first preferred, but when the Humber pattern machines did well on the path and

proved easier on hills these came to the fore. However their advantage going uphill was reversed when descending as the weight was taken off the hind wheel and they could become unsteerable, so by 1884 the Cripper pattern had become predominant.

The Humber Cripper tricycle, named after the racing man R. Cripps, was the definitive machine with the steering direct, that is by handles directly connected to the front axle and not via rods or levers. By that time tandems, where the riders sat one behind the other, usually with the lady in front, were beginning to replace the old sociable side-by-sides.

The Quadrant Tricycle Company, with their own patented remote-steering arrangement for the front wheel, remained successful whilst resisting the direct-steering vogue until the end of the era. Out of step with fashion, the Quad-

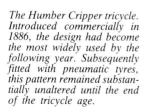

The Humber Cripper tricycle. Introduced commercially in 1886, the design had become the most widely used by the following year. Subsequently fitted with pneumatic tyres, this pattern remained substantially unaltered until the end of the tricycle age.

LEFT: *The Olympia tandem tricycle was introduced by Marriott and Cooper in 1887 and employed the direct steering of the Humber type. Ladies sat at the front as it was considered unseemly for them to face a gentleman's rear. The pneumatic tyres date this example after 1890.*

RIGHT: *A Quadrant tricycle. With a similar wheel layout to the Cripper but with its own distinctive remote steering arrangement, the somewhat old-fashioned Quadrant retained its adherents and was consistently successful.*

rant was widely accepted as the safest and steadiest touring machine on the market.

Pneumatic tyres were introduced in 1889 but by then the tricycle was losing ground to the safety, which was found to be lighter and easier running. By the mid 1890s tricycles had lost the battle and continued principally as delivery vehicles and specialised sporting machines, although children's tricycles remained popular until the 1950s and infants' tricycles are still widely available today.

Because of the difficulties in storing tricycles only a small number have survived and this rarity is reflected in their value to collectors today.

SAFETIES, SPRING FRAMES AND PNEUMATICS

The concept of a bicycle driven through gears via a chain to the rear wheel had been discussed in the pages of *The English Mechanic* as far back as 1869, even before the Ordinary had arrived. In 1879, with the Ordinary in its heyday, one of the largest manufacturers, the Tangent and Coventry Tricycle Company, introduced the Bicyclette. This was a small-wheeled machine (40 inches, 1 m, front; 24 inches, 610 mm, rear) with chain drive to the rear wheel and raked front forks. They promised 'perfect safety in mounting and dismounting; a steel steed that will be pronounced the most comfortable and tempting amongst steel steeds'. Initial press comments were encouraging, but the public refused to be tempted; it appeared that improvements in safety were not to be traded for reductions in speed or handling quality. From this distance the Bicyclette appears

remarkably similar to the Rover which finally proved such a success six years later. Perhaps its failure was simply due to poor marketing, for no professionals were employed to break records on it. Whatever the reason, it was dropped from the catalogue in 1881.

Despite this reverse the subject of safety would not go away and the continued favour enjoyed by the Facile and the Xtraordinary led several makers to introduce rear-driven safety machines in 1884. Among these was the Rover of Sutton and Starley (J. K. Starley was a nephew of James Starley). He showed the Rover in February 1885 at the Stanley Bicycle Club Show. It was not immediately acclaimed, indeed there were substantial early modifications to be made to the steering arrangement, but in September of that year, with a professional rider, it established a new record

The Bicyclette. Invented by Harry Lawson in 1879, this machine shows how designers were thinking even at the height of the Ordinary era. Although the public did not accept it, or indeed any rear-driven machines, for a further six years, it established a new word in the French language.

The Rover safety, introduced in 1884 by John Kemp Starley, finally established the modern cycle. No examples of the first two patterns of the Rover have survived, and by the autumn of 1885 the cumbersome remote steering had been replaced by direct steering. This early Rover is on display in the Science Museum, London.

A Whippet of the late 1880s. This curious anti-vibration machine may look odd but is a pleasant riding bicycle and much prized among collectors.

24

A cross-frame safety bicycle, about 1886. This machine is representative of the many hundreds of models of cross-framed machines of the late 1880s. Without a maker's badge they are difficult to attribute with certainty.

for one hundred miles (160 km). Sales soared at once and other makers rushed to bring out their own copies for the following season. The Rover sales literature proclaimed that it 'set the fashion to the world' and for once this was no exaggeration. It certainly created a fervour of experimentation and invention that within five years had established the final pattern for the two-wheeled machine.

The original Rover frame was simply derived from that of the Ordinary, but with two additional pairs of stays to support the saddle and chainwheel it formed the diamond shape which was to become universal. Paradoxically, after other makers had standardised on the stayed diamond frame with a seat tube, J. K. Starley still favoured the more elaborate curved tubes and an open frame.

There were many experiments with cross-frame patterns which had a diagonal tube running from the head to the rear hub and an upright tube supporting the saddle and the bottom bracket, but difficulties in keeping the chain tensioned eventually led to their demise in favour of the diamond pattern. The introduction of safety machines brought a new population into bicycling and the period 1885-9 produced immense variation in machines. Exhibitors at the Stanley Show rose from 287 to 1564 in six years.

Whilst faster than the Ordinary and of course safer, the new machines were by no means as comfortable. Sprung saddles were tolerable but the vibration through the handles was disagreeable. Thus for a few short seasons before the introduction of the pneumatic tyre, inventors worked on grafting ingenious anti-vibration de-

This ladies' Rover of 1889 illustrates the weakness of the diamond frame when the top tube is removed to accommodate the lady's skirt. It has a plunger brake, which continued in use on pneumatic tyres, and foot rests for coasting.

A diamond-framed Humber safety with cushion tyres, dating from the early 1890s. By this time the frame design had been resolved and only brakes and gearing systems were lacking to complete the modern cycle.

vices into the frames and front forks. Of these perhaps the Whippet had the most elegant solution and it is still a most pleasurable machine to ride. The vibration problem was happily solved by John Boyd Dunlop's invention of the pneumatic tyre. First used in a race in May 1889, the pneumatic was at first expensive and cushion tyres were a cheaper alternative, but by 1895 the solid-tyred bicycle had gone and the modern bicycle had become established.

The year 1896 produced a spectacular boom in cycle production, led by fashionable society. Profiteering flotations encouraged wild overproduction and shoddy quality. This inevitably led to an equally dramatic collapse the following year. However the bicycle had become a working man's necessity, not simply a means of recreation, and the process of refinement and improvement continued year by year.

ACCESSORIES

by Peter W. Card

Accessories fall into a number of categories and the most popular then, as with collectors today, were the various forms of lighting equipment. Oil lamps were used almost exclusively until the mid 1890s. It would seem that the first lamp to be advertised specifically for the bicycle was an unnamed example fitted as standard equipment on the Phantom velocipede in 1869. However the first commercially successful oil lamp was made particularly for the Ordinary bicycle from about 1876. Like later varieties which were made until 1894, they were called 'hub lamps' because they were fitted through the spokes of the large front wheel and clamped around the hub. While the wheel was in motion the lamp stayed central and vertical as the bicycle hub spun inside the top of the lamp with the metal being protected by leather bearings.

Although the firm of Salsbury claims to have invented the hub lamp it was Joseph Lucas of Birmingham who developed it in 1878. Termed the 'simple-style', his hub lamp did not have a wick winding mechanism but relied upon the use of a stout pin to pick the wick out of the wick tube collar. It was accurately trimmed with a sharp knife before lighting. In about 1880 a second type of hub lamp appeared called the divided style. This was much larger in size as well as oil carrying capacity and the lamp was manufactured in two halves and hinged at the top, thus providing a narrower profile to insert between the spokes. After entry into the wheel it was simply dropped over the hub with front and rear halves clipping together at the base. By 1882 both styles of hub lamp featured mechanical wick winders so the job of adjusting the wick, although still awkward, made lighting and trimming the lamp much easier.

With the introduction of rear-driving safety bicycles in about 1886 came the safety (oil) head lamp. This style of lamp was stark and austere in appearance like the hub lamp, but had a parallel-sprung bracket at the rear. This served to help prevent the flame being extinguished by the vibration as the solid tyres negotiated pot holes and stones. They were made in various styles by at least two dozen manufacturers in Britain alone, including firms like Powell and Hanmer, H. Miller and W. Bown.

The introduction of pneumatic tyres around 1891 meant that there was less vibration so it was found there was no longer a need to retain a large wick and a high volume of circulating air just to keep the lamp alight. Lamps became smaller and neater and various methods were patented to project the light forward, rather than just reflect the flame through a plain bevelled glass.

Charles E. Challis started founding bells for Ordinaries and tricycles in 1882. At first they were similar to small cow bells and rang continuously, hanging from the handle bars. As the selling point of a bicycle bell was the power to alert, bells gradually increased in size and loudness to 'make the deafest creature jump'. This expression from a mid 1880s advertisement would not have appealed to the majority of other road users, who had little respect for bicyclists at this time.

In 1887 Joseph Lucas introduced a model which was subsequently imitated by other manufacturers. The Number 42 was termed a combination bell because it combined a choice of continuous or single ringing, the latter being activated by a striking lever as with modern bells. With

LEFT: *(From back left to right) A divided-style hub lamp by Joseph Lucas, about 1882; a simple-style hub lamp manufactured by T. S. Tongue with the cheaper type of centralising antennae; Boys and Rucker made cyclometers from the middle 1880s — this example rings a bell at the completion of every mile; a whistle retailed by J. A. Knox; a watch which had to be firmly attached to the handlebars.*

RIGHT: *(Rear) A road map of the Reading area dating from 1889; a cycle catalogue would include several pages of assorted accessories; (front, from left to right) a sandwich box of 1885; a cheap continuous alarm bell by Challis; an oil-burning lamp made by Rea Neale and Bourne for tricycles; a spirit bottle of 1885; a Salsbury lamp made in 1890 for a safety bicycle; a Lucas Number 42c combination bell of about 1889.*

the advent of a smoother ride after the introduction of pneumatic tyres the 'continuous ringer' was of little use and was dropped from accessory catalogues by 1894.

Whistles are no longer associated with cycling and were never so popular or as practical as bells. They were worn strung on to a lanyard and hung around the neck and it must have been a very brave Ordinary rider who actually let go of the handle bars when negotiating a corner to put the whistle in his mouth!

The bugle is now considered part of cycling's heritage and it might be assumed that many enthusiastic cyclists and tricyclists possessed one. In fact it was usually only the Club Captain and Sub-Captain who used them although many splendidly engraved and decorated examples still survive. Each club had its own arrangement of calls which could be sounded should it be necessary, for example, to check furious riding or change riding formation while out on a club tour.

There were many other interesting accessories introduced during this period including dress clips for lady riders, tool rolls, cyclometers, maps and snack companions.

VETERAN CYCLE CLUBS

Anyone seriously interested in early bicycles should consider joining a club. This gives the opportunity of riding different machines, the most satisfactory way of learning about them. Many clubs have machines available for loan to members. Apply to the club secretaries below.

Belvoir Bicyclists: Mr T. Skeet, De La Forge, Stone Bit Lane, Marston, Grantham, Lincolnshire NG32 2JH.

Benson Veteran Cycle Club: Mrs C. N. Passey, The Bungalow, 61 Brook Street, Benson, Oxfordshire OX9 6LH. Telephone: 0491 38414.

Boston Veteran Bicycle Club: Mrs Beryl Page, Ivy Cottage, London Road, Frampton, Lincolnshire PE22 1BP.

Bygone Bykes: Mr A. C. Stephenson, 16 Crossgates Avenue, Leeds LS15 7QQ.

Desford Lane Pedallers: Mr A. H. C. Pickering, 29 The Coppice, Narborough, Leicestershire LE9 5FB. Telephone: 0533 841881.

Long Sutton and District Veteran Cycle Club: Miss Nicola Wellband, 136 Spalding Road, Pinchbeck, Spalding, Lincolnshire PE11 3VE. Telephone: 0775 723941.

March Veteran and Vintage Cycle Club: Mrs M. Bedford, 1 Norwood Avenue, March, Cambridgeshire PE15 8LT.

Northleach OTW: Mr W. B. Robinson, The Firs, 10 Shepherds Way, Northleach, Gloucestershire GL54 3ED.

Peterborough Veteran Cycle Club: Mrs J. Denton, 10 All Saints Close, Asfordby, Leicestershire LE14 3TF. Telephone: 0664 813151.

Solent Veteran Bicycle and Tricycle Club: Mr R. Safe, 26 Rimington Road, Cowplain, Portsmouth, Hampshire PO8 8UA. Telephone: 0705 264800.

Veteran Cycle Club: Honorary Secretary, Michael Morgan, 129 Radlett Road, Frogmore, Park Street, St Albans, Hertfordshire AL2 2LA.

Honorary secretaries of local sections of the Veteran Cycle Club.

Chiltern: Geoff Paine, 31 Yorke Road, Croxley Green, Rickmansworth, Hertfordshire WD3 3DW.

Essex: Chris Rich, Soller, The Green, Blackmore, Ingatestone, Essex CM4 0RT.

Lancashire: Frank Evans, 163 Hoyles Lane, Cottam, Preston, Lancashire PR4 0NB.

Midlands: Frank Prickett, 89 Great Stone Road, Northfield, Birmingham B31 2LT.

North-west: Paul Adams, 264 The Glen, Runcorn, Cheshire WA7 2TF.

North Road: Frank Turner, 51 Bowershott, Letchworth, Hertfordshire SG6 2EU.

Ripley Road (Surrey): Les Bowerman, Send Manor, Ripley, Surrey GU23 6JS.

Scotland: Eric Wishart, 69 Promenade, Portobello, Edinburgh EH15 2DX.

South-western: Peter Soper, 29 Nursery End, Pilton, Barnstaple, Devon EX31 1RA.

Sussex: Maggie Tyhurst, 108 Brighton Road, Newhaven, East Sussex BN9 9NS.

International Veteran Cycle Association: Mrs V. Dalzell, 22 Woodbank Road, Groby, Leicestershire LE6 0BN.

'Wheeling' magazine of November 1885 pictured the Kangaroo dwarf front-driver racing with the Rover. The Rover is already half a wheel in front; within three years it had completely ousted its rival.

FURTHER READING

Books published by the Pinkerton Press, 522 Holly Lane, Erdington, Birmingham B24 9LY, are available from the publishers or from the CTC Shop, 69 Meadrow, Godalming, Surrey GU7 3HS.

Adams, G. Donald. *Collecting and Restoring Antique Bicycles.* Tab Books Incorporated.

Bartleet, H. W. *Bartleets Bicycle Book,* 1931. Pinkerton Press, reprinted 1983.

Griffin, H. H. *Bicycles and Tricycles of the Year 1889.* Reprinted by the Pinkerton Press.

Griffin, H. H. *Bicycles of the Year 1877.* Reprinted by the Pinkerton Press.

McGurn, James. *On Your Bicycle.* John Murray, 1987.

Sturmeys Indispensable Handbook to the Safety Bicycle 1885. Pinkerton Press, reprinted.

The Velocipede 1869. Pinkerton Press, reprinted.

Whitt, F. R. *The Restoration of Veteran Cycles.* Pinkerton Press.

The following books are out of print but well worth seeking out.

Griffin, H. H. *Cycles and Cycling.* George Bell, 1890.

Hillier, G. Lacy. *The Badminton Library: Cycling.* Longmans Green, 1887.

Richie, Andrew. *King of the Road.* Wildwood House, 1975.

Wilkinson-Latham, Robert. *Cycles in Colour.* Blandford Press, 1978.

The Boneshaker is published three times a year by the Veteran Cycle Club, free to members.

The Bartleet Collection in the Coventry Central Library, Smithfold Way, Coventry CV1 1FY (telephone: 0203 832314) has the best and most accessible collection of early bicycle books and periodicals.

PLACES TO VISIT

Major collections are marked with an asterisk. In all cases intending visitors are advised to find out times of opening before making a special journey.

Abingdon Museum, County Hall, Market Place, Abingdon, Oxfordshire OX14 3HA. Telephone: 0235 523703.

* *Alec Brown Collection*, Drumlanrig Castle, near Thornhill, Dumfries. Telephone: 03685 226.

Alnwick Castle Museum of Antiquities, Alnwick Castle, Alnwick, Northumberland NE66 1NQ. Telephone: 0665 510777.

* *Automobilia Transport Museum*, Billy Lane, Old Town, Hebden Bridge, West Yorkshire HX7 8RY. Telephone: 0422 844775.

Beamish: The North of England Open Air Museum, Beamish Hall, Beamish, Stanley, County Durham DH9 0RG. Telephone: 0207 231811.

* *Birmingham Museum of Science and Industry*, Newhall Street, Birmingham B3 1RZ. Telephone: 021-235 1661.

Blake Museum, Blake Street, Bridgwater, Somerset. Telephone: 0278 456127.

Blake's Lock Museum, Gasworks Road, Reading, Berkshire RG1 3DH. Telephone: 0734 390918.

Bradford Industrial Museum, Moorside Road, Eccleshill, Bradford, West Yorkshire BD2 3HP. Telephone: 0274 631756.

Bridewell Museum of Norwich Trades and Industries, Bridewell Alley, Norwich, Norfolk NR2 1AQ. Telephone: 0603 667228.

Brighton Art Gallery and Museum, Church Street, Brighton, East Sussex BN1 1UE. Telephone: 0273 603005.

Bristol Industrial Museum, Prince's Wharf, Prince Street, Bristol, Avon BS1 4RN. Telephone: 0272 251470.

Brooklands Museum, The Clubhouse, Brooklands Road, Weybridge, Surrey KT13 0QN. Telephone: 0932 857381.

Buckinghamshire County Museum, Church Street, Aylesbury, Buckinghamshire HP20 2QP. Telephone: 0296 88849.

Peter Card Collection of Cycle Lighting, 54 Willian Way, Letchworth, Hertfordshire SG6 2HL. Telephone: 0462 675117.

Cheltenham Art Gallery and Museum, Clarence Street, Cheltenham, Gloucestershire GL50 3JT. Telephone: 0242 237431.

* *Christchurch Tricycle Museum*, Quay Road, Christchurch, Dorset BH23 1BY. Telephone: 0202 479849.

Cothey Bottom Heritage Centre, Brading Road, Ryde, Isle of Wight. Telephone: 0983 568431.

Cotswolds Motor Museum, The Old Mill, Bourton-on-the-Water, Gloucestershire GL54 2BY. Telephone: 0451 821255.

Cusworth Hall Museum, Cusworth Lane, Doncaster, South Yorkshire DN5 7TU. Telephone: 0302 782342.

Derby Industrial Museum, The Silk Mill, off Full Street, Derby DE1 3AR. Telephone: 0332 255309.

Donington Collection, Donington Park, Castle Donington, Derby DE7 2RP. Telephone: 0332 810048.

Dorman Museum, Linthorpe Road, Middlesbrough, Cleveland TS5 6LA. Telephone: 0642 813781.

Dover Transport Museum, Connaught Road, Dover, Kent. Telephone: 0304 840563.

Dumfries Museum, The Observatory, Church Street, Dumfries DG2 7SW. Telephone: 0387 53374.

Ely Museum, High Street, Ely, Cambridgeshire CB5 8HZ. Telephone: 0353 666655.

* *Erddig*, near Wrexham, Clwyd LL13 0YT. Telephone: 0978 355314.

Folk Museum of West Yorkshire, Shibden Hall, Halifax, West Yorkshire HX3 6XG. Telephone: 0422 352246.

Gladstone Court, Biggar, Lanarkshire ML12 6DT. Telephone: 0899 21050.

* *Glasgow Museum of Transport*, Kelvin Hall, 1 Bunhouse Road, Glasgow G3 8DP. Telephone: 041-357 3929.

Gray Art Gallery and Museum, Clarence Road, Hartlepool, Cleveland TS24 8BT. Telephone: 0429 268916.

Gunnersbury Park Museum, Gunnersbury Park, London W3 8LQ. Telephone: 081-992 1612.

Gwent Rural Life Museum, The Malt Barn, New Market Street, Usk, Gwent NP5 1AU. Telephone: 0291 673777.

Hereford and Worcester County Museum, Hartlebury Castle, Hartlebury, near Kidderminster, Worcestershire DY11 7XZ. Telephone: 0299 250416.

Horsham Museum, Causeway House, 9 The Causeway, Horsham, West Sussex RH12 1HE. Telephone: 0403 254959.

Peter Hoyte Collection, Millbridge, Farnham, Surrey. Telephone: 025279 3373.

Hull and East Riding Museum, 36 High Street, Hull, North Humberside HU1 1EP. Telephone: 0482 593902.

Kelham Island Industrial Museum, Alma Street, Sheffield S3 8RY. Telephone: 0742 722106.

* *Warren Kern Collection*, 16 Colquitt Street, Liverpool L1 4DG. Telephone: 051-709 4252.

* *Knutsford Courtyard Coffeehouse*, 92 King Street, Knutsford, Cheshire WA16 6ED. Telephone: 0565 653974.

Lakeland Motor Museum, Holker Hall, Cark in Cartmel, Grange-over-Sands, Cumbria LA11 7PL. Telephone: 05395 58509.

Leicestershire Museum of Technology, Abbey Pumping Station, Corporation Road, Abbey Lane, Leicester. Telephone: 0533 661330.

Liverpool Museum, William Brown Street, Liverpool L3 8EN. Telephone: 051-207 0001 or 5451.

* *Mark Hall Bicycle Museum*, Muskham Road, Harlow, Essex CM18 6YL. Telephone: 0279 439680.

Mechanical Musical and Doll Collection, Church Road, Portfield, Chichester, West Sussex PO19 4HN. Telephone: 0243 785421.

Melrose Motor Museum, Annay Road, Melrose, Roxburghshire TD6 9LW. Telephone: 089628 2624.

Monkwearmouth Station Museum, North Bridge Street, Sunderland, Tyne and Wear SR5 1AP. Telephone: 091-567 7075.

* *Alex Moulton Ltd*, The Hall, Bradford-on-Avon, Wiltshire. Telephone: 0225 862991.

Museum of British Road Transport, St Agnes Lane, Hales Street, Coventry, West Midlands CV1 1PN. Telephone: 0203 832425.

* *Museum of Historic Cycling*, The Old Station, Camelford, Cornwall PL32 9TZ. Telephone: 0840 212811.

Museum of Lakeland Life and Industry, Abbot Hall, Kendal, Cumbria LA9 5AL. Telephone: 0539 722464.

Museum of Lincolnshire Life, The Old Barracks, Burton Road, Lincoln LN1 3LY. Telephone: 0522 528448.

Myreton Motor Museum, Aberlady, East Lothian EH32 0PZ. Telephone: 08757 288.

* *National Cycle Museum*, The Lawn, Union Road, Lincoln LN1 3BU. Telephone: 0522 545091.

National Motor Museum, John Montagu Building, Beaulieu, Hampshire SO42 7ZN. Telephone 0590 612345.

Nottingham Industrial Museum, Courtyard Buildings, Wollaton Park, Nottingham NG8 2AE. Telephone: 0602 284602.

Oakhill Manor Museum, Oakhill, Bath, Avon. Telephone: 0749 840210.

* *Oswestry Bicycle Museum*, 11 Arthur Street, Oswestry, Shropshire.

* *Ned Passey Collection*, 61 Brook Street, Benson, Oxfordshire OX9 6LH. Telephone: 0491 38414.

Perth Museum and Art Gallery, George Street, Perth PH1 5LB. Telephone: 0738 32488.

* *Pinkerton Collection*, Arbury Hall, Nuneaton, Warwickshire. Telephone: 0676 40529.

Rotherham Museum, Clifton Park, Rotherham, South Yorkshire S65 2AA. Telephone: 0709 382121.

Royal Museum of Scotland, Chambers Street, Edinburgh EH1 1JF. Telephone: 031-225 7534.

Salford Museum and Art Gallery, Peel Park, The Crescent, Salford, Lancashire M5 4WU. Telephone: 061-736 2649.

* *Science Museum*, Exhibition Road, South Kensington, London SW7 2DD. Telephone: 071-938 8000.

* *Science Museum Store*, Wroughton Aerodrome, Swindon, Wiltshire SN4 9NS. Telephone: 0793 814816.

Shuttleworth Collection, Old Warden Aerodrome, Biggleswade, Bedfordshire SG18 9EP. Telephone: 0767 627288.

* *Snowshill Manor*, near Broadway, Worcestershire WR12 7JU. Telephone: 0386 852410.

Social History Museum, Holy Trinity Church, Trinity Street, Colchester, Essex CO1 1JN. Telephone: 0206 712942.

Somerset County Museum, Taunton Castle, Castle Green, Taunton, Somerset TA1 4AA. Telephone: 0823 255504.

Stanford Hall Motorcycle Museum, Stanford Hall, Lutterworth, Leicestershire LE17 6DH. Telephone: 0788 860250.

Swansea Museum, Victoria Road, Swansea, West Glamorgan SA1 1SN. Telephone: 0792 653763.
Tolson Memorial Museum, Ravensknowle Park, Huddersfield, West Yorkshire HD5 8DJ. Telephone: 0484 541455 or 530591.
Totnes Motor Museum, Steamer Quay, Totnes, Devon TQ9 5AL. Telephone: 0803 862777.
Turton Tower, Chapeltown Road, Bromley Cross, near Bolton, Lancashire BL7 0HG. Telephone: 0204 852203.
Tyrwhitt-Drake Museum of Carriages, Mill Street, Maidstone, Kent. Telephone: 0622 754497.
* *Ulster Folk and Transport Museum*, Cultra Manor, Holywood, County Down, Northern Ireland BT18 0EU. Telephone: 0232 428428.
Warrington Museum and Art Gallery, Bold Street, Warrington, Cheshire WA1 1JG. Telephone: 0925 30550.
Warwickshire County Museum, Market Place, Warwick CV34 3SA. Telephone: 0926 412021.
Welsh Folk Museum, St Fagans, Cardiff, South Glamorgan CF5 6XB. Telephone: 0222 569441.
Weybridge Museum, Church Street, Weybridge, Surrey KT13 8DE. Telephone: 0932 843573.
Williamson Art Gallery and Museum, Slatey Road, Oxton, Birkenhead, Merseyside L43 4UE. Telephone: 051-652 4177. The Baxter Collection.
Woodspring Museum, Burlington Street, Weston-super-Mare, Avon BS23 1PR. Telephone: 0934 621028.
York Castle Museum, The Castle, Tower Street, York YO1 1RY. Telephone: 0904 853611.

HOLLAND
Rijksmuseum Paleis Het Loo, Koninklijk Park 1, 7315 JA Apeldoorn. Telephone: 055 212244.
* *Velorama*, Waalkade 107, 6511 XR Nijmegen. Telephone: 080 225851.

FRANCE
* *Musée de Velo*, Couvent de l'abbaye de Cadouin, 24480 Buisson-de-Cadouin, Lozére. Telephone: 53 23 95 46.
* *Musée de la Commanderie*, Viapres-le-Petit, 10380 Placy l'Abbaye. Telephone: 25 37 70 30.
* *Musée de l'Automobile de Bretagne*, 40 route de Fougères, 35510 Cesson-Sevigné. Telephone: 90 62 00 17.
* *Musée du Cyclisme*, 40240 Labastide-d'Armagnac, Landes. Telephone: 58 44 80 52.
* *Musée Vivant de la Bicyclette*, Bourguenolles, 50800 Villedieu-les-Poêles, Manche. Telephone: 33 61 13 90.
* *Musée de la Moto et du Velo*, Château de Lunéville, 54300 Lunéville, Meurthe-et-Moselle. Telephone: 83 74 07 20.
* *Musée National de la Voiture et de Tourisme*, Château de Compiègne, 60200 Compiègne, Oise. Telephone: 44 40 04 37.
* *Musée Barthelemy Thimonier*, place de l'Hôtel de Ville, 69550 Amplepuis, Rhône. Telephone: 74 89 08 90.
* *Musée de l'Automobile Henri Malartre*, Château de Rochetaillée, 60270 Fontaines-sur-Saône, Rhône. Telephone: 78 22 18 80.
* *Musée de l'Automobile du Mans*, circuit des 24 Heures, rue du Panorama, 72000 le Mans, Sarthe. Telephone: 43 72 50 60.

There are good collections in Germany at Einbeck, Munich, Neckarsulm, Berlin, Dresden and Donaueschingen; in Switzerland at Lucerne; in Austria at Vienna; and in the Czech Republic at Prague.

UNITED STATES OF AMERICA
* *The Bicycle Museum of America*, North Pier, 435 East Illinois Street, Chicago, Illinois 60611.
* *The Burgwardt Bicycle Museum*, 3943 North Buffalo Road, Orchard Park, New York 14127.
* *Henry Ford Museum*, 20900 Oakwood Boulevard, Dearborn, Michigan 48121.

JAPAN
* *Bicycle Culture Centre*, Jitenshakaikan No 3 Building, 1-9-3 Akasaka Minato-ku, Tokyo.

AUSTRALIA
* *Canberra Bicycle Museum*, 2 Badham Street, Dickson, ACT 2602.
* *White House Collection*, Highway 1, Westbury, Tasmania.
* *Queen Victoria Museum*, Wellington Street, Launceston, Tasmania 7250.